YOUR KNOWLEDGE HAS VALUE

Jiyi Tian

Database of Auto Parts Warehouse Design

GRIN Publishing

Bibliographic information published by the German National Library:

The German National Library lists this publication in the National Bibliography; detailed bibliographic data are available on the Internet at http://dnb.dnb.de .

Imprint:

Copyright © 2011 GRIN Verlag, Open Publishing GmbH
Print and binding: Books on Demand GmbH, Norderstedt Germany
ISBN: 978-3-656-11153-5

This book at GRIN:

http://www.grin.com/en/e-book/187359/database-of-auto-parts-warehouse-design

GRIN - Your knowledge has value

Since its foundation in 1998, GRIN has specialized in publishing academic texts by students, college teachers and other academics as e-book and printed book. The website www.grin.com is an ideal platform for presenting term papers, final papers, scientific essays, dissertations and specialist books.

Visit us on the internet:

http://www.grin.com/

http://www.facebook.com/grincom

http://www.twitter.com/grin_com

Content

1. Description of the application and its users

The database designed for AutoParts Warehouse is to mainly serve as an ecommerce website. Customer can register online with their shipping address and transaction information. Customer can search the parts they need from company website and place order. According to the order come from customer, company can ship the parts to correspondent customers. In order to make economy efficient, company won't save too many parts in stock. Oppositely, Company will keep only minimum number of each part. If one of parts runs out of stock, a staff will order the part from vendor and then send it to customer. Our scope will mainly cover the function of customer order, price query, parts summary and company stock. Online transaction with bank and shipment with shipping company are out of our scope.

1.1 User (Predefined and Specified in Section 6):

a. **Web Customers**

b. **Customer Represents**

c. **Customer Managers**

d. **Database Administrator**

1.2 Process

a. **Create/Edit Customer**

   User: Customer

   Data I/O: Customer Information Input

b. **Query parts by correspondent car type**

   User: Customer/Staff

   Data I/O: Search criteria input and display output

c. **Place Order**

   User: Customer

   Data I/O: Purchase Information Input

d. **Edit Order**

   User: Customer/Represents (Staff)

Data I/O: Data change input and display corrected information

e. Add/Edit Product

User: Staff

Data I/O: Product Information Input and display output

f. Update Inventory

User: Staff

Data I/O: Corrected Information Input

g. Stock

User: Staff (Manager)

Data I/O: Stock Information Input

h. Query parts and vendors Information

User: Staff

Data I/O: parts and vendors query criteria input and display output

i. Query Customer Order Information

User: Customer/Staff

Data I/O: Customer, parts and data info input and display output

j. Query Staff stock information

User: Staff (Manager)

Data I/O: Parts and Staff information input and display output

1.3 Data Flow of Diagram of Database design

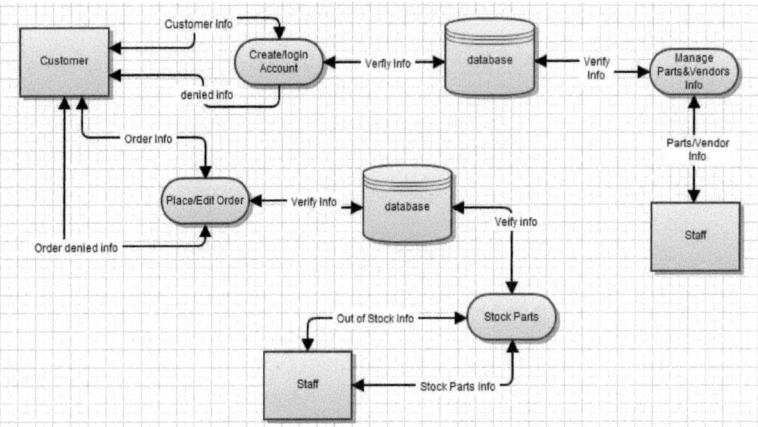

1.4 Scope Define:

Our scope will mainly cover the function of customer order, price query, parts summary and parts stock. Online transaction with bank and shipment with shipping company are out of our scope.

1.5 Assumptions

- All type of Car has been listed in Car Table

- Original Price comes from vendor will not change by time

- Each part can only be suitable for one type of car

2. Conceptual and physical design of your database

Based on I/O needs I defined in the section 1. In section 2, I create the Entity Relationship Diagram and explain the all relationship. Tables detail will be listed with SQL script in the Appendix I.

Database of Auto Parts Warehouse Design

2.1 Entity Relationship Diagram

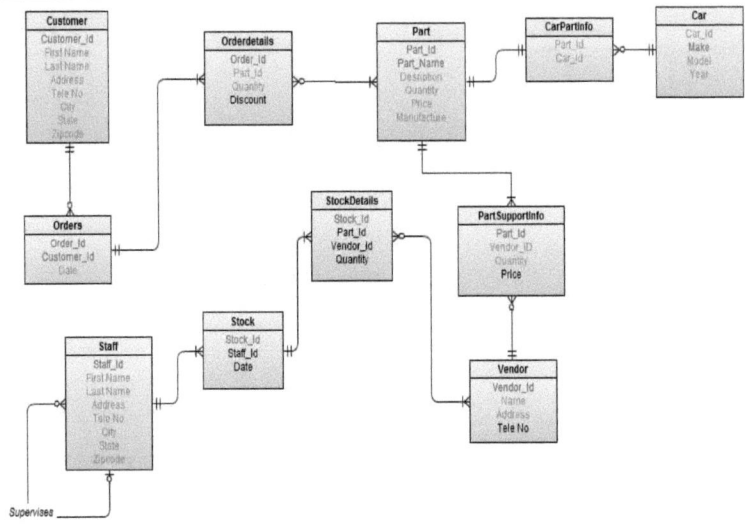

Entity Relationship Diagram (ERD)

2.2 Relationship Explanation

Customer-Orders:

A customer can have zero or many orders and each order should belong to one customer.

Orders-Orderdetails

An order can possess at least one details such as one order can purchase two or more parts. Orderdetail should belong to one order

Orderdetails-Part

An orderdetails can have one or more parts and one part can be belong to zero of more orderdetails

Part-CarPartInfo

This is one on one mandatory relationship

Car-CarPartInfo

Database of Auto Parts Warehouse Design

Car table contain the information of all car in the market. Car can possess zero or more part in our store. However, one part must be only suitable for one type of car

Staff-Manager

A staff should be supervised by only one manager and one manager can supervise zero or more staff

Staff-Stock

One staff can create zero or more stock and one stock order should belong to one staff

Stock-Stockdetails

One stock order can have many stockdetails, while one stockdetails can only belong to one stock

Stockdetails-Vendor

One stockdetials can be related to one or more vendors, because one part can be offered by different vendors. A vendor can have zero or more stockdetails.

Vendor-PartSupportInfo

A Vendor can offer zero of more parts. And a part should be offered at least one Vendor.

Part-PartSupportInfo

PartSupportInfo should belong to only one part. And, Part have own at least one of many PartSupportInfo

3. Explanation of transactions that impact the database and their SQL implementation

Process1 a): Create Customer

Transaction Name: CreateCustomer

In this transaction, database will create new customer and automatically assign unique ID to the customer.

SQL Implementation:

```
BEGIN TRANSACTION
SET TRANSACTION ISOLATION LEVEL READ COMMITTED
INSERT INTO Customer Values
('ID','firstname','lastname','Address','teleNo','Email','City','Stat
e','Zip')
COMMIT TRANSACTION
```

Process1 b): Edit Customer

Transaction Name: EditCustomer

In this transaction, database will execute update statement to update date of correspondent customer. Only Customer have the right to change its account information

SQL Implementation:

```
BEGIN TRANSACTION
SET TRANSACTION ISOLATION LEVEL READ COMMITTED
UPDATE Customer SET First_Name='firstname' where Cid='12'
COMMIT TRANSACTION
```

Process 2: Place order

Transaction Name: PlaceOrder

In this transaction, database will insert a new recode in 'Order' table and 'Orderdetails' tables, and update the data of Quantity in the 'Part' table. If there is any error happens, transaction will rollback.

SQL Implementation:

```
CREATE PROC PlaceOrder
@Oid as int,
@Pid as int,
@Cid as int,
```

```
@Quantity as int,
@date as date,
@total as int
as
set nocount on
    select @total= SUM(Quantity) from Orderdetail od,Orders o
    where od.Oid=o.Oid and Cid=@Cid and Pid=@Pid and date=@date
  IF ((@total+@Quantity)<10)
  Begin
        insert into Orders Values (@Oid,@Cid,@date)
        insert into dbo.Orderdetail Values
    (@Oid,@Pid,@Quantity,Null)
        update Part set Onhand=Onhand-@Quantity
  End
  Else
  print 'Over days limit'
```

Process 3: Edit order

Transaction Name: EditOrder

In this transaction, database will update the data in 'Order','Part' and 'Orderdetails' table, if there is any error happens, transaction will rollback.

SQL STATEMENT:

Reference to Process 2

Process 4 a): Add part

Transaction Name: AddPart

In this transaction, database will insert new recode to the 'Part' table and Car table

SQL STATEMENT:

```
CREATE PROC AddPart
@Pid as int,
@Part_Name as nvarchar(30),
@Onhand as int,
@Price as real,
@Manufacture as nvarchar(50),
@Car_Id as int
as
set nocount on
Begin TRANSACTION
insert into Part values
(@Pid,@Part_Name,Null,@Onhand,@Price,@Manufacture)
insert into CarPartInfo values (@Pid,@Car_Id)
if (@@ERROR<>0) ROLLBACK TRANSACTION
COMMIT
```

Process 4 b): Edit Part

Transaction Name: EditPart

In this transaction, database will update the information of 'Part' table.

SQL STATEMENT:

```
BEGIN TRANSACTION
SET TRANSACTION ISOLATION LEVEL READ COMMITTED
UPDATE Part SET Description='Description...'
COMMIT TRANSACTION
```

Process 6: Stock

Transaction Name: Stock

In this transaction, database will insert new record of 'Stock' table and 'Stockdetails' table, and update Part table

SQL STATEMENT:

```
CREATE PROC AddNewStock
@Staff_Id as int,
@Stock_Id as int,
@Data as date,
@Pid as int,
@Vid as int,
@Quantity as int,
@Origin_Price as real
as
set nocount on
Begin transaction
insert into Stock values (@Stock_Id,@Staff_Id,@Data)
insert into Stockdetail
values(@Stock_Id,@Pid,@Vid,@Quantity,@Origin_Price)

Commit
```

Process 7: Query Parts and Vendors information

Transaction Name: QueryPrt&VensInfo

In this transaction, database will display the parts and related vendors and can compare the different price come from different vendors for a given part.

SQL STATEMENT:

```
BEGIN TRANSACTION
SET TRANSACTION ISOLATION LEVEL READ COMMITTED
select v.Name,p.Part_Name,ps.Origin_Price
from Vendor v,Part p,PartSupportInfo ps
where p.Pid=ps.Pid and v.Vid=ps.Vid
Order by v.Name
COMMIT TRANSACTION
```

Process 8: Query Customer Order information

Transaction Name: QueryCustOrdInfo

In this transaction, database will display a given customer and all the orders has been placed.

SQL STATEMENT:

```
CREATE PROC findCustOrder
@Cid as int,
@datein as date,
@dateout as date
as
set nocount on
select Last_Name, Part_Name,od.Quantity,DATE from Customer c,Orders
o,Orderdetail od,Part p
where c.Cid=O.Cid and o.Oid=od.Oid and od.Pid=p.Pid and o.Date
between @datein and @dateout
Go
```

Process 9: Query Staff stock information

Transaction Name: QueryStafStocInfo

In this transaction, database will query the stock information according to staff.

SQL STATEMENT:

```
BEGIN TRANSACTION
SET TRANSACTION ISOLATION LEVEL READ COMMITTED
select Last_Name, Part_Name, p.Pid, sd.Quantity
from Stock st, Stockdetail sd, Staff s, Part p
where st.Staff_Id=s.Staff_Id and sd.Stock_id=st.Stock_Id and
sd.Pid=p.Pid
Order by Last_Name
COMMIT TRANSACTION
```

4. Documentation of all integrity rule

4.1 Primary and Foreign key

4.2 Customer, Staff, Part, Vendor name cannot be null

Set not null constraint of all above attribute or use SQL:

ALTER TABLE Customer ADD CONSTRAINT Not Null (First_Name, Last_Name)

4.3 Email must be unique

Set unique constraint of attribute or use SQL:

ALTER TABLE Customer ADD CONSTRAINT emailUnique Unique(Email)

4.4 Price and Quantity should be larger than 0

Set constraint price should be larger than 0 and Quantity should be equal or larger than 0

4.5 When manager stock new part from vendor, the inventory number (Onhand) in Part table and the quantity in the PartSupportInfo table should be updated correspondently

Use trigger 1:

```
create trigger InventoryBalCheck on Stockdetail for update
as
begin
      declare @Pid as int
      declare @Quantity as int
      declare @Vid as int
      declare @OriginPrice as real
      declare @Result as nvarchar(260)
      select @Pid=pid,@Quantity=Quantity,@Vid=Vid from inserted
      update Part set Onhand=Onhand+@Quantity where Pid=@Pid
      select @Result from PartSupportInfo where Pid=@Pid and
      @Vid=Vid
      IF (@Result IS NOT Null)
      BEGIN
            update PartSupportInfo set
            Quantity=Quantity+@Quantity where Vid=@Vid and
            Pid=@Pid
      END
      Else
      BEGIN
            Insert into PartSupportInfo VALUES
            (@Pid,@Vid,@Quantity,@OriginPrice)
      END
END
```

4.6 When manage stock new part, the part id and vendor id should be on the part list and vendor list

Use trigger 2:

```
create trigger PartVendorChek on Stockdetail for update, Insert
as
begin
      declare @Pid as int
      declare @Quantity as int
      declare @Vid as int
      declare @OriginPrice as real
      declare @PResult as nvarchar(260)
      declare @VResult as nvarchar(260)
      select@Pid=pid,@Quantity=Quantity,@Vid=Vid,@OriginPrice=Ori
      gin_Price from inserted
      select @PResult from Part where Pid=@Pid
      select @VResult from Vendor where Vid=@Vid
      IF ((@PResult is Null) OR(@VResult is Null))
      Begin
            ROLLBACK TRANSACTION
            Print 'Vendor id or Part id is not on the list'
      End
      Else Print 'Transaction OK'
END
```

4.7 When updating CarPartInfo table Car ID should be on the list of Car table

Use trigger 3:

```
create trigger CarIdCheck on CarPartInfo for insert
as
begin
      declare @Pid as int
      declare @Car_Id   as int
      declare @result as nvarchar(260)
      select @result=Car_Id from Car where Car_Id=@Car_Id
      if (@result is Null)
      Begin
      ROLLBACK TRANSACTION
      Print 'Car_Id is invalid'
      End

END
```

4.8 Each Customer can only purchase same part less than 10 within same day

Use Store Procedure:

```
CREATE PROC PlaceOrder
@Oid as int,
@Pid as int,
@Cid as int,
@Quantity as int,
@date as date,
@total as int
as
set nocount on
        select @total= SUM(Quantity) from Orderdetail od,Orders o
        where od.Oid=o.Oid and Cid=@Cid and Pid=@Pid and date=@date
        IF ((@total+@Quantity)<10)
        Begin
                insert into Orders Values (@Oid,@Cid,@date)
                insert into dbo.Orderdetail Values
        (@Oid,@Pid,@Quantity,Null)
                update Part set Onhand=Onhand-@Quantity
        End
        Else
        ROLLBACK TRANSACTION
        print 'Over days limit'
```

5. Documentation of all queries

Query1. List any customer's order in a given period

```
CREATE PROC findCustOrder
@Cid as int,
@datein as date,
@dateout as date
as
set nocount on
select Last_Name, Part_Name,od.Quantity,DATE from Customer c,Orders
o,Orderdetail od,Part p
where c.Cid=O.Cid and o.Oid=od.Oid and od.Pid=p.Pid and o.Date
between @datein and @dateout
Go
```

Query2. List the sales number of all parts and order by descendant

```
select Part_Name, SUM(od.Quantity) sales_number
from Orderdetail od, Part p
where od.Pid=p.Pid
group by Part_Name
Order by sales_number
```

Query3. Display the net profit within a given period

```
CREATE PROC calNetProfit
@datein as date,
@dateout as date
as
set nocount on
select SUM((Price-Origin_Price)*od.Quantity) as NetProfit
from Part p,Orderdetail od,PartSupportInfo ps, Orders o
where p.Pid=ps.Pid and p.Pid=od.Pid and od.Oid=o.Oid
and o.Date between @datein and @dateout
Group by p.Pid
Go
```

Query4. List all parts whose inventory less than 3

```
select Part_Name, Onhand
from Part
where Onhand<=3
```

Query5. List Vendors and all parts it offered with original price

```
select v.Name,p.Part_Name,ps.Origin_Price
from Vendor v,Part p,PartSupportInfo ps
where p.Pid=ps.Pid and v.Vid=ps.Vid
Order by v.Name
```

Query6. List information of staff and stock

```
select Last_Name, Part_Name, p.Pid, sd.Quantity
from Stock st, Stockdetail sd, Staff s, Part p
where st.Staff_Id=s.Staff_Id and sd.Stock_id=st.Stock_Id and
sd.Pid=p.Pid
Order by Last_Name
```

Query7. Calculate the average amount of consumption of each customer

```
select c.Cid, AVG(Price*od.Quantity) as AmtOfConsumption
from Customer c,Part p,Orders o,Orderdetail od
where c.Cid=o.Cid and o.Oid=od.Oid and od.Pid=p.Pid
Group by c.Cid
```

Query8. List managers and correspondent staff supervised

```
select s1.Manager_Id, s1.Staff_Id, s1.Last_Name
from Staff s1,Staff s2
where s1.Staff_Id=s1.Manager_Id
```

Query9. List a given manufacture and all parts of it.

```
CREATE PROC ListManuParts
@Manufacture as nvarchar(20)
as
set nocount on
select Manufacture,Part_name,Description from Part
where Manufacture=@Manufacture
```

6. Documentation of users and their role

6.1 Web Customer

Customer can create and edit its own accounts on our website and browser every parts sold on website by part name or type of car.

6.2 Customer Represent

Customer Represent can inspect each customer's orders and when needed, contact with customer via email. In addition, customer represent can only read part information when needed and report the manager about the low inventory level.

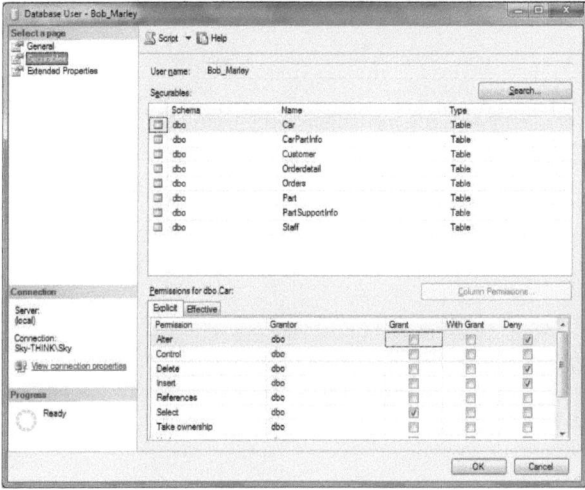

6.3 Staff Manager

Manager inherent all function of customer represent. Besides, Manager has the right to place discount on customer orders and stock new parts when its inventory level low

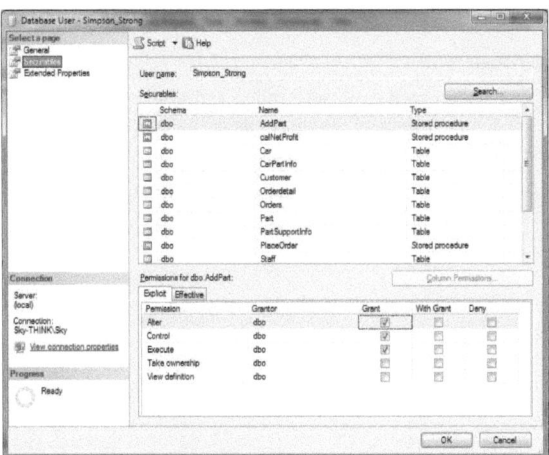

6.4 Database Administrator

DBA have the right to manage database such as change database structure or add/delete tables in the database and etc.

7. Documentation of test result

Testing contains three parts, functional test, data integrity test and server user test. The purpose of testing is to verify whether all target functions and data integrity are achieved or not, and find the drawbacks in current system and provide solution in the future.

7.1 Data integrity test

1) Vendor name Not Null constraint

SQL: insert into Vendor values (4,null,'44 Kalamani Rd','4567896785')

> Messages
>
> Msg 515, Level 16, State 2, Line 1
> Cannot insert the value NULL into column 'Name', table 'AutoPartsWarehouse.dbo.Vendor'; column does not allow nulls.
> The statement has been terminated.

2) Customer Email should be unique

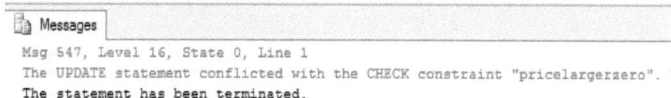

Cid	First_Name	Last_Name	Address	TeleNo	Email	City
1	Steve	Lee	NULL	3522784567	Lee@gmail.com ...	NULL
2	Allen	Lin	NULL	8053456789	lin@gmail.com	NULL

SQL: update Customer set Email='lin@gmail.com' where Last_Name='Lee'

> Messages
>
> Msg 2627, Level 14, State 1, Line 1
> Violation of UNIQUE KEY constraint 'emailUnique'. Cannot insert duplicate key in object 'dbo.Customer'.
> The statement has been terminated.

3) Price should larger than 0 and Quantity should equal or larger than 0

SQL: Update Part set Price=0 where Pid=1

> Messages
>
> Msg 547, Level 16, State 0, Line 1
> The UPDATE statement conflicted with the CHECK constraint "pricelargerzero". '
> The statement has been terminated.

SQL: Update Part set Onhand= -1

> Messages
>
> Msg 547, Level 16, State 0, Line 1
> The UPDATE statement conflicted with the CHECK constraint "quantitycheck". '
> The statement has been terminated.

4) A. Test trigger 1 Insert new Stock order

```
exec AddStock 3,5,'2011-12-06',1,1,3,250

/*Quantity is 3;Vid is 1and Pid is 1. Expect transaction ok
and Part and PartSupportInfo table should be updated*/
```

Part,PartSupportInfo Table Before:

	Pid	Vid	Quantity	Origin_Price			
1	1	1	2	250			

	Pid	Part_Name	Description	Onhand	Price	Manufacture
1	1	Front_Bumper	for audi 2010	4	299.99	CROWN

Part,PartSupportInfo Table After:

	Pid	Vid	Quantity	Origin_Price
1	1	1	5	250

	Pid	Part_Name	Description	Onhand	Price	Manufacture
1	1	Front_Bumper	for audi 2010	7	299.99	CROWN

B. Test trigger 2 when Vid and Pid not on exist list

```
exec AddStock 3,7,'2011-12-07',1,25,5,250
/*Part id 25 5 is invalid expect transaction rollback*/
```

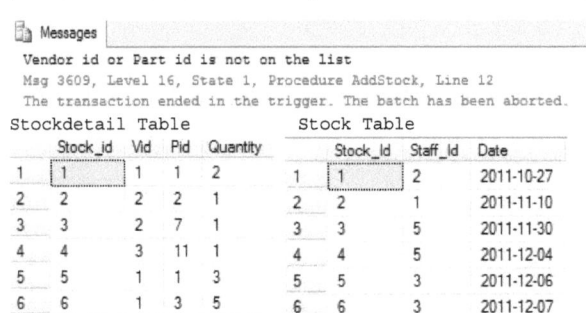

```
Messages
Vendor id or Part id is not on the list
Msg 3609, Level 16, State 1, Procedure AddStock, Line 12
The transaction ended in the trigger. The batch has been aborted.
```

Stockdetail Table

	Stock_jd	Vid	Pid	Quantity
1	1	1	1	2
2	2	2	2	1
3	3	2	7	1
4	4	3	11	1
5	5	1	1	3
6	6	1	3	5

Stock Table

	Stock_Id	Staff_Id	Date
1	1	2	2011-10-27
2	2	1	2011-11-10
3	3	5	2011-11-30
4	4	5	2011-12-04
5	5	3	2011-12-06
6	6	3	2011-12-07

Transaction has been terminated and no new rows been inserted into Stock and Stockdetail tables

C. Test trigger 3, Car_Id should be valid when execute add Part procedure

20

Database of Auto Parts Warehouse Design

```
exec AddPart 20,'Rear Bumper',2,250,'Crown',5

/*here car_id 5 is invalid expect transaction rollback*/
```

📋 Messages

```
Car_Id is invalid
Msg 3609, Level 16, State 1, Procedure AddPart, Line 12
The transaction ended in the trigger. The batch has been aborted.
```

7.2 Functional test

1) Test place order

```
exec PlaceOrder 14,12,1,20,'2011-12-06'

/*Quantity number is 20, more than 10, expect transaction abort*/
```

📋 Messages

```
Over days limit or over inventory
```

```
exec PlaceOrder 14,12,1,4,'2011-12-06'
/*Quantity number is 4, more than 10, expect transaction ok*/
```

📋 Messages

```
Command(s) completed successfully.
```

📰 Results	📋 Messages				📰 Results	📋 Messages	
	Oid	Pid	Quantity	Discount		Oid	Cid	Date
6	6	11	1	NULL	6	6	1	2011-10-23
7	7	12	5	NULL	7	7	3	2011-10-30
8	8	7	4	0.9	8	8	11	2011-11-10
9	9	1	1	NULL	9	9	11	2011-11-11
10	10	2	1	NULL	10	10	5	2011-11-15
11	11	4	1	NULL	11	11	6	2011-11-20
12	12	3	1	0.75	12	12	4	2011-11-29
13	13	6	1	NULL	13	13	7	2011-12-02
14	14	12	4	NULL	14	14	1	2011-12-06

12	Gas_Cap	... for VW 2011	... 11	13.49	STANT
12	Gas_Cap	... for VW 2011	... 7	13.49	STANT

```
exec PlaceOrder 15,12,1,6,'2011-12-06'
/*Quantity number is 6, leads customer 1 purchase more than 10
part_id 12, expect transaction abort*/
```

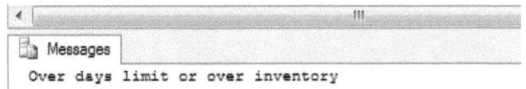

2) Test stock order:

```
exec AddStock 3,5,'2011-12-06',1,1,3,250
```

```
/*expert new information added in stock and stockdetail table
and part and partsupportinfo will be also updated by trigger*/
```

Stockdetail table

Stock_id	Vid	Pid	Quantity	Origin_Price
5 5	1	1	3	240

Stock table

Stock_Id	Staff_Id	Date
5 5	3	2011-12-06

The trigger test for updating correspondent information in
part and partsupportinfo table, please see trigger test 7.1.4

3) Add Part

```
exec AddPart 13,'Body Kit',0,550,'Coupe',1
/*expect new part information added into part table
```

Part table

Pid	Part_Name	Description	Onhand	Price	Manufacture
13 13	Body Kit	NULL	0	550	Coupe

CarPartInfo table:

Pid	Car_Id
11 11	8
12 12	17
13 13	1

4) Query for calculating net profit on each part

```
exec calNetProfit '2011/01/01','2011/12/31'
```

Database of Auto Parts Warehouse Design

```
/*expect list the correspondent part id and net profit in
given period*/
```

	pid	NetProfitBypart
1	1	332.94
2	2	79.99
3	3	679.92
4	4	79.99
5	5	59.99
6	6	99.99
7	7	319.96
8	10	499.99
9	11	200.99
10	12	107.82

5) List customer order

```
exec findCustOrder 1,'2011/01/01','2011/12/31'
/*list all the customer order with customer name and part name
and quantity*/
```

	Last_Name	Part_Name	Quantity	DATE
4	Roddick	Engine	1	2011-10-13
5	Lin	Head_Lights	1	2011-10-18
6	Lee	Suspension	1	2011-10-23
7	diesel	Gas_Cap	5	2011-10-30
8	Xu	Hood	4	2011-11-10
9	Xu	Front_Bumper	1	2011-11-11
10	Brooke	Front_Bumper	1	2011-11-15
11	Young	Head_Lights	1	2011-11-20
12	Kohl	Front_Bumper	1	2011-11-29
13	Clooney	Hood	1	2011-12-02
14	Lee	Gas_Cap	4	2011-12-06

8. Disaster recovery plan of AutoParts Warehouse

Considering the size and loading of AutoParts Warehouse database, I choose the backup strategy of a combination of full and T-log backup with different time period. And, Consider the data in CarList and PartList Table are rarely changed, I also adopted differential backup for security. In addition, due to the hardware limit, we cannot support running two SQL server instances so that I won't provide mirroring for database recovery. Following contains backup and restore procedure, and backup and restore strategy.

8.1 Create T_SQL statement for backup and restore

1) Acquire file directory of SQL Server

```
create function f_getdbpath(@dbname sysname){…}
```

2) SQL statement for backup

```
create proc p_backupdb
```

a. Full backup

```
exec p_backupdb@bkpath='c:\',@bkfname='db_\DATE\_db.bak'
```

b. Differential backup

```
exec
p_backupdb@bkpath='c:\',@bkfname='db_\DATE\_df.bak',@bktype
='DF'
```

c. T-log backup

```
Exec
p_backupdb@bkpath='c:\',@bkfname='db_\DATE\_log.bak',@bktyp
e='LOG'
```

3) SQL statement for recovery

```
create proc p_RestoreDb
```

a. Full restore

```
exec p_RestoreDb
@bkfile='c:\db_20111204_db.bak',@dbname='db'
```

b. Differential restore

```
exec p_RestoreDb
@bkfile='c:\db_20111204_db.bak',@dbname='db',@retype='DBNOR
'
exec p_backupdb
@bkfile='c:\db_20111204_df.bak',@dbname='db',@retype='DF
```

    c. T-log restore

```
exec p_RestoreDb
@bkfile='c:\db_20111204_db.bak',@dbname='db',@retype='DBNOR
'
exec p_backupdb
@bkfile='c:\db_20111204_log.bak',@dbname='db',@retype='LOG'
```

8.2 Backup Strategy

    a. Full Backup once a week at Sunday(22:00)

    b. Differential backup once a day(20:00)

    c. T-log backup every 2 hours

9. Documentation of the data warehouse and its purpose

AutoParts data warehouse contains two subset areas, inventory statistic and order geographic distribution which are described in the following sections. Additionally, the data warehouse contains views that are used to support the data mining scenarios that are described later in this topic. The purpose to create this data warehouse is to find the optimal inventory pattern in order to keep lower running cost. And find the distribution of customer geographically for optimizing the establishment of actual part warehouse in the future.

9.1 Inventory statistic

- Contains the inventory data according to the time period

- Contains the inventory data according the related auto parts

9.2 Geographic Information

- Contains the address and area data from customer

- Contains the order quantity from customer

9.3 Data Mining Scenarios

The trending in the AutoParts database supports the following data mining scenarios:

Forecasting: Support analyst to investigate the change of parts inventory pattern by time and region

Actual warehouse analysis: Support analyst to find the best warehouse location distribution

Database of Auto Parts Warehouse Design

Market basket analysis: Supports the scenario of a developer creating a market basket solution that suggests a product based on other products that already exist in a customer's shopping cart.

Appendix I – SQL Script of all tables

- ● **Part**

```
CREATE TABLE [dbo].[Part](
     [Pid] [int] NOT NULL,
     [Part_Name] [nchar](30) NULL,
     [Description] [nchar](30) NULL,
     [Onhand] [int] NULL,
     [Price] [real] NULL,
     [Manufacture] [nvarchar](50) NULL,
 CONSTRAINT [PK_Part] PRIMARY KEY CLUSTERED
(
     [Pid] ASC
)WITH (PAD_INDEX  = OFF, STATISTICS_NORECOMPUTE  = OFF, IGNORE_DUP_KEY
= OFF, ALLOW_ROW_LOCKS  = ON, ALLOW_PAGE_LOCKS  = ON) ON [PRIMARY]
) ON [PRIMARY]

GO

ALTER TABLE [dbo].[Part]  WITH CHECK ADD  CONSTRAINT [pricelargerzero]
CHECK  (([Price]>(0)))
GO

ALTER TABLE [dbo].[Part] CHECK CONSTRAINT [pricelargerzero]
GO

ALTER TABLE [dbo].[Part]  WITH CHECK ADD  CONSTRAINT [quantitycheck]
CHECK  (([Onhand]>=(0)))
GO

ALTER TABLE [dbo].[Part] CHECK CONSTRAINT [quantitycheck]
GO
```

- ● **Car**

```
CREATE TABLE [dbo].[Car](
     [Car_Id] [nchar](10) NOT NULL,
     [Make] [nchar](10) NULL,
     [Model] [nchar](10) NULL,
     [Year] [nchar](10) NULL,
 CONSTRAINT [PK_Car] PRIMARY KEY CLUSTERED
(
     [Car_Id] ASC
)WITH (PAD_INDEX  = OFF, STATISTICS_NORECOMPUTE  = OFF, IGNORE_DUP_KEY
= OFF, ALLOW_ROW_LOCKS  = ON, ALLOW_PAGE_LOCKS  = ON) ON [PRIMARY]
) ON [PRIMARY]

GO

CarPartInfo

CREATE TABLE [dbo].[CarPartInfo](
     [Pid] [int] NOT NULL,
     [Car_Id] [nchar](10) NOT NULL,
 CONSTRAINT [PK_CarPartInfo] PRIMARY KEY CLUSTERED
```

```
(
      [Pid] ASC
)WITH (PAD_INDEX  = OFF, STATISTICS_NORECOMPUTE  = OFF, IGNORE_DUP_KEY
= OFF, ALLOW_ROW_LOCKS  = ON, ALLOW_PAGE_LOCKS  = ON) ON [PRIMARY]
) ON [PRIMARY]

GO


ALTER TABLE [dbo].[CarPartInfo]  WITH CHECK ADD  CONSTRAINT
[FK_CarPartInfo_Car] FOREIGN KEY([Car_Id])
REFERENCES [dbo].[Car] ([Car_Id])
GO

ALTER TABLE [dbo].[CarPartInfo] CHECK CONSTRAINT [FK_CarPartInfo_Car]
GO

ALTER TABLE [dbo].[CarPartInfo]  WITH CHECK ADD  CONSTRAINT
[FK_CarPartInfo_Part] FOREIGN KEY([Pid])
REFERENCES [dbo].[Part] ([Pid])
GO


ALTER TABLE [dbo].[CarPartInfo] CHECK CONSTRAINT [FK_CarPartInfo_Part]
GO
```

- **Customer**

```
CREATE TABLE [dbo].[Customer](
      [Cid] [int] NOT NULL,
      [First_Name] [nchar](10) NULL,
      [Last_Name] [nchar](10) NULL,
      [Address] [nchar](30) NULL,
      [TeleNo] [nchar](10) NULL,
      [Email] [nchar](20) NULL,
      [City] [nchar](15) NULL,
      [State] [nchar](10) NULL,
      [Zip] [nchar](10) NULL,
 CONSTRAINT [PK_Customer] PRIMARY KEY CLUSTERED
(
      [Cid] ASC
)WITH (PAD_INDEX  = OFF, STATISTICS_NORECOMPUTE  = OFF, IGNORE_DUP_KEY
= OFF, ALLOW_ROW_LOCKS  = ON, ALLOW_PAGE_LOCKS  = ON) ON [PRIMARY],
 CONSTRAINT [emailUnique] UNIQUE NONCLUSTERED
(
      [Email] ASC
)WITH (PAD_INDEX  = OFF, STATISTICS_NORECOMPUTE  = OFF, IGNORE_DUP_KEY
= OFF, ALLOW_ROW_LOCKS  = ON, ALLOW_PAGE_LOCKS  = ON) ON [PRIMARY]
) ON [PRIMARY]
```

- **Orderdetail**

```
CREATE TABLE [dbo].[Orderdetail](
      [Oid] [int] NOT NULL,
      [Pid] [int] NOT NULL,
      [Quantity] [int] NULL,
```

```
       [Discount] [real] NULL,
 CONSTRAINT [PK_Orderdetail] PRIMARY KEY CLUSTERED
(
       [Oid] ASC,
       [Pid] ASC
)WITH (PAD_INDEX  = OFF, STATISTICS_NORECOMPUTE  = OFF, IGNORE_DUP_KEY
= OFF, ALLOW_ROW_LOCKS  = ON, ALLOW_PAGE_LOCKS  = ON) ON [PRIMARY]
) ON [PRIMARY]

GO


ALTER TABLE [dbo].[Orderdetail]  WITH CHECK ADD   CONSTRAINT
[FK_Orderdetail_Order] FOREIGN KEY([Oid])
REFERENCES [dbo].[Orders]  ([Oid])
GO

ALTER TABLE [dbo].[Orderdetail] CHECK CONSTRAINT [FK_Orderdetail_Order]
GO

ALTER TABLE [dbo].[Orderdetail]  WITH CHECK ADD   CONSTRAINT
[FK_Orderdetail_Part] FOREIGN KEY([Pid])
REFERENCES [dbo].[Part]  ([Pid])
GO

ALTER TABLE [dbo].[Orderdetail] CHECK CONSTRAINT [FK_Orderdetail_Part]
GO
```

● **Orders**

```
CREATE TABLE [dbo].[Orders](
       [Oid] [int] NOT NULL,
       [Cid] [int] NOT NULL,
       [Date] [date] NULL,
 CONSTRAINT [PK_Order] PRIMARY KEY CLUSTERED
(
       [Oid] ASC
)WITH (PAD_INDEX  = OFF, STATISTICS_NORECOMPUTE  = OFF, IGNORE_DUP_KEY
= OFF, ALLOW_ROW_LOCKS  = ON, ALLOW_PAGE_LOCKS  = ON) ON [PRIMARY]
) ON [PRIMARY]

GO


ALTER TABLE [dbo].[Orders]  WITH CHECK ADD   CONSTRAINT
[FK_Order_Customer] FOREIGN KEY([Cid])
REFERENCES [dbo].[Customer]  ([Cid])
GO

ALTER TABLE [dbo].[Orders] CHECK CONSTRAINT [FK_Order_Customer]
GO
```

● **PartSupportInfo**

```
CREATE TABLE [dbo].[PartSupportInfo](
       [Pid] [int] NOT NULL,
```

```
        [Vid] [int] NOT NULL,
        [Quantity] [nchar](10) NULL,
        [Origin_Price] [real] NULL,
 CONSTRAINT [PK_PartSupportInfo_1] PRIMARY KEY CLUSTERED
(
        [Pid] ASC,
        [Vid] ASC
)WITH (PAD_INDEX  = OFF, STATISTICS_NORECOMPUTE  = OFF, IGNORE_DUP_KEY
= OFF, ALLOW_ROW_LOCKS  = ON, ALLOW_PAGE_LOCKS  = ON) ON [PRIMARY]
) ON [PRIMARY]

GO


ALTER TABLE [dbo].[PartSupportInfo]  WITH CHECK ADD  CONSTRAINT
[FK_PartSupportInfo_Part] FOREIGN KEY([Pid])
REFERENCES [dbo].[Part] ([Pid])
GO


ALTER TABLE [dbo].[PartSupportInfo] CHECK CONSTRAINT
[FK_PartSupportInfo_Part]
GO


ALTER TABLE [dbo].[PartSupportInfo]  WITH CHECK ADD  CONSTRAINT
[FK_PartSupportInfo_Vendor1] FOREIGN KEY([Vid])
REFERENCES [dbo].[Vendor] ([Vid])
GO


ALTER TABLE [dbo].[PartSupportInfo] CHECK CONSTRAINT
[FK_PartSupportInfo_Vendor1]
GO
```

- **Staff**

```
CREATE TABLE [dbo].[Staff](
        [Staff_Id] [int] NOT NULL,
        [First_Name] [nchar](10) NULL,
        [Last_Name] [nchar](10) NULL,
        [ManagedBy] [int] NULL,
        [Address] [nchar](10) NULL,
        [TeleNo] [nchar](10) NULL,
        [City] [nchar](10) NULL,
        [State] [nchar](10) NULL,
        [Zip] [nchar](10) NULL,
 CONSTRAINT [PK_Staff] PRIMARY KEY CLUSTERED
(
        [Staff_Id] ASC
)WITH (PAD_INDEX  = OFF, STATISTICS_NORECOMPUTE  = OFF, IGNORE_DUP_KEY
= OFF, ALLOW_ROW_LOCKS  = ON, ALLOW_PAGE_LOCKS  = ON) ON [PRIMARY]
) ON [PRIMARY]

GO


ALTER TABLE [dbo].[Staff]  WITH CHECK ADD  CONSTRAINT [FK_Staff_Staff]
FOREIGN KEY([ManagedBy])
REFERENCES [dbo].[Staff] ([Staff_Id])
```

```
GO

ALTER TABLE [dbo].[Staff] CHECK CONSTRAINT [FK_Staff_Staff]
GO
```

- **Stock**

```
CREATE TABLE [dbo].[Stock](
      [Stock_Id] [int] NOT NULL,
      [Staff_Id] [int] NULL,
      [Date] [date] NULL,
 CONSTRAINT [PK_Stock] PRIMARY KEY CLUSTERED
(
      [Stock_Id] ASC
)WITH (PAD_INDEX  = OFF, STATISTICS_NORECOMPUTE  = OFF, IGNORE_DUP_KEY
= OFF, ALLOW_ROW_LOCKS  = ON, ALLOW_PAGE_LOCKS  = ON) ON [PRIMARY]
) ON [PRIMARY]

GO

ALTER TABLE [dbo].[Stock]  WITH CHECK ADD  CONSTRAINT [FK_Stock_Staff]
FOREIGN KEY([Staff_Id])
REFERENCES [dbo].[Staff] ([Staff_Id])
GO

ALTER TABLE [dbo].[Stock] CHECK CONSTRAINT [FK_Stock_Staff]
GO
```

- **StockDetail**

```
CREATE TABLE [dbo].[Stockdetail](
      [Stock_id] [int] NOT NULL,
      [Vid] [int] NOT NULL,
      [Pid] [int] NOT NULL,
      [Quantity] [int] NOT NULL,
      [Origin_Price] [real] NULL,
 CONSTRAINT [PK_Stockdetail_1] PRIMARY KEY CLUSTERED
(
      [Stock_id] ASC,
      [Vid] ASC
)WITH (PAD_INDEX  = OFF, STATISTICS_NORECOMPUTE  = OFF, IGNORE_DUP_KEY
= OFF, ALLOW_ROW_LOCKS  = ON, ALLOW_PAGE_LOCKS  = ON) ON [PRIMARY]
) ON [PRIMARY]

GO

ALTER TABLE [dbo].[Stockdetail]  WITH CHECK ADD  CONSTRAINT
[FK_Stockdetail_Stock] FOREIGN KEY([Stock_id])
REFERENCES [dbo].[Stock] ([Stock_Id])
GO

ALTER TABLE [dbo].[Stockdetail] CHECK CONSTRAINT [FK_Stockdetail_Stock]
GO

ALTER TABLE [dbo].[Stockdetail]  WITH CHECK ADD  CONSTRAINT
[FK_Stockdetail_Vendor] FOREIGN KEY([Vid])
```

```
REFERENCES [dbo].[Vendor] ([Vid])
GO

ALTER TABLE [dbo].[Stockdetail] CHECK CONSTRAINT [FK_Stockdetail_Vendor]
GO
```

- **Vendor**

```
CREATE TABLE [dbo].[Vendor](
      [Vid] [int] NOT NULL,
      [Name] [nchar](20) NOT NULL,
      [Address] [nchar](10) NULL,
      [TeleNo] [nchar](10) NULL,
 CONSTRAINT [PK_Vendor] PRIMARY KEY CLUSTERED
(
      [Vid] ASC
)WITH (PAD_INDEX = OFF, STATISTICS_NORECOMPUTE = OFF, IGNORE_DUP_KEY
= OFF, ALLOW_ROW_LOCKS = ON, ALLOW_PAGE_LOCKS = ON) ON [PRIMARY]
) ON [PRIMARY]
```